Coffee Cozies

Coffee Cozies

GUILD OF MASTER CRAFTSMAN PUBLICATIONS

First published 2009 by
Guild of Master Craftsman Publications Ltd
Castle Place, 166 High Street,
Lewes, East Sussex BN7 1XU

Reprinted 2010, 2011

Copyright in the Work © GMC Publications Ltd, 2009

ISBN 978-1-86108-646-4

A catalogue record for this book is available from
the British Library.
Charts and pattern checking by Gina Alton

Publisher: Jonathan Bailey
Production Manager: Jim Bulley
Managing Editor: Gerrie Purcell
Senior Project Editor: Virginia Brehaut
Editor: Alison Howard
Managing Art Editor: Gilda Pacitti
Design: Tonwen Jones
Photographer: Laurel Guilfoyle

Set in Gill Sans

Colour origination by GMC Reprographics
Printed and bound in China by Hing Yip Printing
Co. Ltd.

Why we love coffee cozies

FIRST THERE WAS THE TEA COZY, that wonderfully quirky accessory that takes centre stage during the traditional ritual of afternoon tea. Coffee never quite seemed to merit such ceremony. But that was before the world woke up to the taste and smell of real coffee. No longer satisfied with the harsh little granules, whose only connection with coffee seemed to be a word on a jar, we began to invest in beans from far-flung places with exotic names that most of us could only dream of visiting. Suddenly, such exotic delights as Jamaican Blue Mountain, Monsoon Malabar and the deeply-seductive sounding Dark Italian were rubbing shoulders on the shelf with the tea caddy.

The first example of a coffee jug incorporating a plunger dates from 1850s France, though the Italians also claim to have invented the method. Whatever its provenance, and whether they call it a French press, a plunge filter or a cafetiere, many people believe this simple, efficient piece of kit is the best way to preserve the flavour of their coffee.

But this growing love for real coffee presented a problem: without that fancy covering that adorned the teapot, the coffee jug seemed naked and functional. What was needed, in order to brighten up our new best beverage, was the coffee cozy. When *Knitting* magazine ran a competition asking its creative readers to design their own, entries flooded in. So many, in fact, that we decided to put the best into this book. So, put on the kettle, unleash the fresh aroma of your coffee – and knit up your favourite cozy.

Emma Kennedy
Editor
Knitting magazine

Contents

Two sets of instructions are given for these simple cozies by Frankie Brown, to suit two different yarns. Each produces a stunning and effortless rainbow effect as you knit – the choice is yours!

Rainbow rib

Materials

Noro Kureyon 100% wool (109yds/100m per 50g ball)

1 x 50g ball in shade 154

A pair of 4.5mm (US7:UK7) needles

4 x ⅗in (1.5cm) buttons

Darning needle

Alternative yarn (shown on pages 12–13):

Noro Silk Garden Lite (125m/136yds per 50g)

1 x 50g ball in shade 2014

A pair of 3.75mm (US5:UK9) needles

4 x ⅗in (1.5cm) buttons

Tension

Kureyon: 24 sts and 31 rows to 4in (10cm) over patt using 4.5mm needles

Silk Garden Lite: 30 sts and 36 rows to 4in (10cm) over patt using 3.75mm needles

Use larger or smaller needles to achieve correct tension

Method

These rainbow rib cozies are knitted from top to bottom in a stitch known as mistake rib, with added button band tabs. Instructions are given for Noro Kureyon, with variations in brackets for Noro Silk Garden Lite.

Main piece

Cast on 55 (67) sts.
Work 50 (60) rows in mistake rib, slipping the first st of each row k-wise.

Mistake rib pattern

Every row: (k2, p2) to last 3 sts, k2, p1.
Cast off in patt.

Top and bottom button tabs

With RS facing pick up and k4 (6) sts at the top or bottom of one side of the cozy and knit 5 (7) rows.
Cast off.

Centre button tab

With RS facing, miss 3 sts after the top band, pick up and k12 (14) sts.
Knit 5 (7) rows.
Cast off.

Buttonhole bands

Kureyon

With RS facing pick up and knit 4 sts at the top or bottom of the other side of the cozy.
Knit 2 rows.
Next row: K2, yf, k2tog.
Knit 2 rows.
Cast off.

Silk Garden Lite

With RS facing pick up and knit 6 sts at the top or bottom of the other side of the cozy.
Knit 3 rows.
Next row: K2, cast off 2, k2.
Next row: K2, cast on 2, k2.
Knit 2 rows.
Cast off.

Middle buttonhole band

Kureyon

With RS facing, miss 3 sts after the bottom band; pick up and knit 12 sts.
Knit 2 rows.
Next row: K3, yf, k2tog, k3, yf, k2tog, k2.
Knit 2 rows.
Cast off.

Silk Garden Lite

With RS facing, miss 3 sts after the bottom band; pick up and knit 14 sts.
Knit 3 rows.
Next row: K3, cast off 2, k4, cast off 2 sts, k3.
Next row: K3, cast on 2, k4, cast on 2 sts k3.
Knit 2 rows.
Cast off.

Making up

Attach buttons. Sew in any loose ends.

The yarn used for this simple design by Charlotte Packham blends from one coffee shade to another, and ribbon detail adds a special touch. Rustic-effect buttons complete the 'country' look of this cozy.

Crème caramel

Materials

Rowan Tapestry DK (approx 120m/131yds per 50g ball)
1 x 50g ball in 170 Country
A pair of 3.5mm (UK9–10:US4) needles
A 3.5mm (UK9:USE4) crochet hook
3 x small buttons
A piece of felt 6¾in x 11¾in (17cm x 30cm)
4 x 14in (36cm) lengths of ½in (1cm) ribbon
Sewing needle and coordinating thread

Tension

25 sts and 34 rows to 4in (10cm) measured over panel patt (12 rows rev st st, 12 rows st st) after blocking, using 3.5mm needles)
Use larger or smaller needles to obtain correct tension

Method

The design is knitted sideways in alternating rows of reverse stocking stitch and stocking stitch, with a border of moss stitch. When casting off, four individual stitches are dropped and unpicked to form ladders for the ribbon to be threaded through. The knitted piece is lined with felt and fastened using buttons and loops.

Cozy

Using 3.5mm needles, cast on 36 sts.
Row 1 (WS): (k1, p1) to end.
Row 2 (RS): (p1, k1) to end.
Row 3: As row 1.
Row 4: As row 2.
Row 5: As row 1.
Row 6: *(p1, k1, p1), p to last 3 sts, (k1, p1, k1).
Row 7: (k1, p1, k1), k to last 3 sts, (p1, k1, p1).
Rows 8–17: Rep rows 6–7 five times more.
Row 18: (p1, k1, p1) k to last 3 sts, (k1, p1, k1).
Row 19: (k1, p1, k1), p to last 3 sts, (p1, k1, p1).
Rows 20–29: Rep rows 18–19 five times more.
Rep from * 3 times more.
Row 102: (p1, k1) to end.

Row 103: (k1, p1) to end.
Row 104: As row 102.
Row 105: As row 103.
Row 106: As row 102.
Row 107: Cast off 4 sts, drop 1 st (take st off the needle) and make 1 ch (crochet-style, using the tips of the needles), cast off 2 sts, drop 1, make 1 ch, cast off 20 sts, drop 1, make 1 ch, cast off 2 sts, drop 1, make 1 ch, cast off final 4 sts.

Making up

Unpick the dropped sts down the piece as far as row 5, creating a 'ladder' effect of four columns. Using needle and thread, secure the loops of the dropped stitches so they unravel no further. Block the piece to the correct measurements of 6¾in x 11¾in (17cm x 30cm).
Using 3.5mm hook, crochet 3 chain loops and attach to the edge, one between each set of ladders and the other in the centre.
Attach buttons to the opposite edge. Thread a piece of coordinating ribbon through each ladder, over the knit sections and through the purl sections, and secure on WS.
Using sewing needle and coordinating thread, line the cozy with the felt.

> ### Tip
> *Stitches may be dropped in different places to create a different pattern.*

Crème caramel chart   *36 sts x 34 rows*

Each square = 1 st and 1 row. Read RS rows from R to L and WS rows from L to R

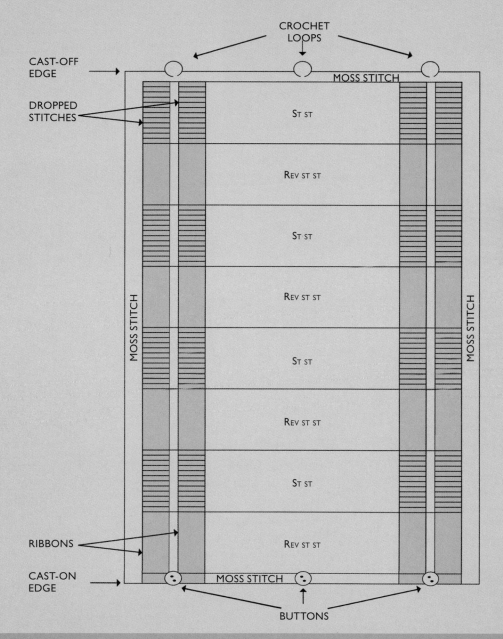

CROCHET LOOPS

CAST-OFF EDGE

DROPPED STITCHES

MOSS STITCH

S*t* st

R*ev* st st

S*t* st

R*ev* st st

MOSS STITCH

S*t* st

R*ev* st st

MOSS STITCH

S*t* st

R*ev* st st

RIBBONS

CAST-ON EDGE

MOSS STITCH

BUTTONS

Knitting and crochet are combined in this flirty design by Margaret Kelleher.
The textured woven stitch is knitted and the frothy frill is crocheted.
Large buttons add a funky finishing touch.

Frothy cream

Materials

Artesano Inca Cloud 100% alpaca
(131yds/120m per 50g ball)
1 x 50g ball in Chocolate
1 x 50g ball in Oatmeal
1 x 50g ball in Cream
A pair of 4mm (US8:UK6) needles
A 4mm (USG/6:UK8) crochet hook
Darning needle
3 x 1⅓in (3.5cm) buttons

Tension

22 sts and 27 rows to 4in (10cm) over basket-weave patt
using 4mm needles, and 12.5 sts and 8 rows (approx) to
4in (10cm) over treble crochet using 4mm hook.
Use larger or smaller needles to achieve correct tension.

Special abbreviation

t-ch = turning chain

Method

The main cozy is knitted sideways with a double crochet border and crochet frill. A treble crochet lining and oversized buttons with chain stitch loops complete the design.

Outer piece

Using 4mm needles and chocolate yarn, cast on 40 sts and work 2 rows in g-st. Work in basket-weave patt until piece measures 11¾in (30cm).

Basket-weave pattern

Rows 1–4: (k2, p2) to end.
Rows 5–8: (p2, k2) to end.
Rep rows 1–8 for patt.
Next row: Knit.
Cast off k-wise and fasten off.

Border

First round: Rejoin chocolate and work a round of dc along one of the short sides, (3dc into corner), dc along the long edge, (3dc into second corner), dc along the other short side, (3dc into third corner), dc along the other long edge, (3dc into fourth corner). Do not break off yarn.

Button loops

(8ch, miss 4ch), 7dc, (8ch, miss 4ch), 7dc, (8ch, miss 4ch).
Note: You may need to adjust the ch length or number of dc worked depending on the size of buttons and the number of dc sts along edge.

Frill

Row 1: Using 4mm hook and oatmeal, work a row of dc along one of the long sides of the chocolate piece.
Rows 2–4: 1ch (t-ch), dc to end.
Row 5: Join in cream and, using 1 strand of cream and 1 strand of oatmeal together, work (6ch, 1dc into first st); * (1dc, 6ch, 1dc) into next st, rep from * to end.
Fasten off.

Lining

Using 4mm hook and cream, begin at short edge opposite the buttonholes and work 1 row dc.
Next row: 2ch, work in treble crochet to end.
Rep last row until lining fits the cozy.
Fasten off.

Making up

Attach the lining to the cozy and sew on the buttons. Sew in any loose ends.

The woven fabric used for this design by Martine Lungley can be worked in any combination of colours. Choose a more dramatic contrast for a more striking effect.

Waffle weave

Materials

Wendy Mode Aran (100m/109yds per 50g ball)
1 x 50g ball in 212 Teal Green (M)
1 x 50g ball in 215 Vapour Blue (C)
A pair of 5mm (US8:UK6) needles
A 5mm (USH/8:UK6) crochet hook
3 x buttons
Darning needle

Tension

20 sts measures 4in (10cm) in width over pattern

Special techniques

Garter stitch (g-st)

Method

This thick, two-tone cover is knitted in one piece in a waffle pattern (two-tone moss stitch) from top to bottom, with just the buttons and loops to sew on afterwards. The four-row pattern uses only one colour at a time so is really easy to work.

Cozy

Using M, cast on 60 sts and work 3 rows g-st.
Work in waffle patt until cozy height measures 6¼in (16cm).

Waffle pattern

Row 1 (RS): Using C, k1, (k1, sl1) to last st, k1.
Row 2: K1, (yf, sl1, yb, k1) to last st, k1.
Using M:
Row 3: K1, (sl1, k1) to last st, k1.
Row 4: K1, (k1, yf, sl1, yb) to last st, k1.
These four rows form the patt and are repeated.
Note: Take care not to pull yarn too tightly when carrying across back of work.
Using M, work 3 rows g-st.
Cast off.

Making up

Press lightly. Sew in ends of yarn. Attach buttons to cozy. Crochet button loops using M and sew on to correspond with buttons.

This reversible design by Bernice Watkins has a nostalgic feel.
An alternative version of the instructions is given for those confident
enough to work in double-sided fairisle.

Retro style

Materials

Any two chunky yarns that produce the correct tension
(one light colour and one dark)
1 x 50g ball in hot pink (A)
1 x 50g ball in burgundy (B)
A pair of 6mm (US10: UK4) needles
2 x ¾in (2cm) poppers or hook-and-eye tape dots
Darning needle

Tension

13 sts and 18.5 rows to 4in (10cm) over patt using
6mm needles
Use larger or smaller needles to achieve correct tension

Special techniques

Double-sided fairisle: (see instructions on page 28)
K2tog cast-off: * k2tog, sl first st over second st; rep from
* to end (using both strands of yarn tog)

Method

This cozy can be worked in traditional fairisle in stocking stitch, joining the two pieces together, or in double-sided fairisle – a more advanced technique that is worked in rib. Poppers or hook-and-eye tape dots are used to fasten it.

Traditional fairisle

Side 1

Using pink, cast on 42 sts.
Foll chart throughout, working pink as main shade and burgundy as contrast. Break off yarn.

Side 2

Using burgundy, cast on 42 sts.
Foll chart again, working burgundy as main colour and pink as contrast. Break off yarn, leaving a long tail for sewing. With wrong sides facing, join the two pieces.

Double-sided fairisle

Cozy

Using one strand of each colour together, cast on 42 sts. Hold both strands of wool as if to knit but use A only to k1, then bring both strands forward as if to purl, but use B only to p1. Bring both strands to back again. Cont to work thus in 1x1 rib, bringing both strands tog forward or back and alternating the colour used (84 sts).

Next row: Cont in rib, working each st in the colour of the row beneath. Foll chart for subsequent rows, working each 'V' in the opposite colour to the background, and remembering that each 'V' represents a pair of sts (front and back) in light and dark shades (a knit stitch and a purl stitch). When you have completed 28 rows, work a k2tog (three-needle) cast-off (see techniques section).

Making up

Attach poppers to the cozy, or use hook-and-eye tape dots.
Darn in any loose ends.

Retro style chart *42 sts x 28 rows*

Each square = 1 st and 1 row

Read RS rows from R to L and WS rows from L to R

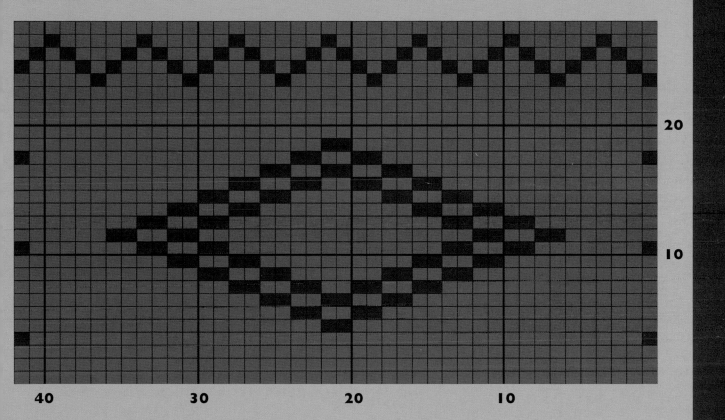

A ███

B ███

Relief stitches worked round the 'posts' of the trebles give a woven look to this simple crocheted design by Pat Strong. The mixture of tones in the yarn enhances the textured effect.

Cotton candy

Tension

Patons Inca (63yds/58m per 50g ball)
1 x 50g ball 7021 Pink Purple Mix or 7004 Red Mix
A 6mm (US10:UK4) crochet hook
3 x buttons
Shirring elastic
Darning needle
Sewing needle

Tension

8.5 sts and 7 rows to 4in (10cm) over patt using 6mm hook
Use larger or smaller hook to achieve correct tension

Special techniques

Front post treble (fptr): Work trebles round the 'post' of the trebles of the previous row from the front of the work
Back post treble (bptr): Work trebles round the 'post' of the trebles of the previous row from the back of the work

Method

This crocheted cozy is worked in one piece from bottom to top, using a combination of front post and back post relief stitches for a 'woven' look. Heart-shaped buttons and shirring-elastic loops are added as fastenings.

Cozy

Using the 6mm crochet hook make 29ch.

Foundation row: Miss 2ch (counts as first st), work 27tr along ch (28 sts).

Row 1: 1ch (t-ch), 4fptr, (4bptr, 4fptr) three times.

Row 2: 1ch (t-ch), 4bptr, (4fptr, 4bptr) three times.

Row 3: As row 2.

Row 4: As row 1.

These four rows form patt.

Rep patt once and fasten off.

Making up

Do not press.

Attach 3 buttons and make loops from shirring elastic to fasten.

Sew in any loose ends.

Crocheted roses adorn this easy garter stitch cozy by Emma Rennie. Two methods of fastening are given: cuff-link style button fastenings or crocheted chains.

Smell the roses

Materials

Twilley's Freedom Spirit (130yds/120m per 50g ball)
1 x 50g ball in 514 Nature (M)
Patons Fairytale Colour 4 Me DK (99yds/90m per 50g ball)
1 x 50g ball in 4981(C)
A pair of 5mm (US6:UK8) needles
A 3.5mm (USE/4:UK9) or 4mm (USG/6:UK8) crochet hook
6 x ¾in (2cm) buttons

Tension

17 sts to 4in (10cm) in width over g-st using 5mm needles
Use larger or smaller needles to achieve correct tension.

Special techniques

Garter stitch (g-st)

Method

A double strand of green random-dyed yarn in garter stitch provides the backdrop for the appliquéd crochet roses. Buttonholes are incorporated so just choose the method of fastening you like best.

Cozy

Using 5mm needles and two strands of M, cast on 29 sts and work 1 row in g-st.

Next row (buttonholes):
K2, (yf, k2tog), k10, (yf, k2tog), k10, (yf, k2tog), k1.

Cont in g-st until work measures 6½in (16.5cm).

Next row: Rep buttonhole row. Work 1 further row in g-st. Cast off.

Roses
Six petals

Make 4ch and join into a ring using a ss. Work 3ch, 11 tr into ring. Join with ss.

Petal row: Work (1ss, 1dc, 1htr, 1tr) into the first treble, then work (1tr, 1htr, 1ss) into the second treble. Repeat until you have worked six petals. Join with ss and fasten off.

Four petals

Make 4ch and join into a ring using a ss. Work 3ch, then 7tr into ring and join with ss.

Petal row: Work exactly as for six-petal flower, forming four petals rather than six. Join with ss and fasten off.

Making up

Press work lightly. Sew in ends. Join buttons in pairs, rather like cufflinks, using a chain of yarn about 1in (2.5cm) long between each button. Layer some four-petal roses on top of six-petal roses to make double flowers. Sew single and double roses randomly over cover.

Tip

If you do not want to use buttons, crochet chains of yarn about 12in (30cm) long, finish with small tassels and use to fasten cover.

Set a table fit for a king with this lovely design by Margaret Yates, which combines yarn in vibrant shades with sumptuous ribbon for a truly regal look.

Royal ribbon

Materials

Louisa Harding Kashmir Aran (83yds/75m per 50g ball)

1 x 50g ball in 9 Red (A)

1 x 50g ball in 10 Purple (B)

Louisa Harding Sari Ribbon (66yds/60m per 50g ball)

1 x 50g ball in 18 Red/Purple (C)

A pair of 5mm (US8:UK6) needles

Darning needle

Tension

19 sts x 24 rows to 4in (10cm) over st st using 5mm needles

Use larger or smaller needles to achieve correct tension

Special techniques

Garter stitch (g-st)

Moss stitch (m-st)

Method

The main cozy is knitted in bands of striped stocking stitch edged in moss stitch. The bands of ribbon yarn begin and end with 'tails' that become tie fastenings for the cozy. An optional garter stitch lining may be knitted and sewn in if desired.

Cozy

Using 5mm needles and yarn C cast on 60 sts leaving a tail of approx 8in (20cm) to be used to tie the finished cozy.
Work 2 rows g-st.
Break off C leaving a tail of approx 8in (20cm).
Join in A and work in st st patt with 3-st m-st borders as folls:

Pattern

Row 1 (WS): *(p1, k1, p1); rep from * to last 3 sts, (p1, k1, p1).
Row 2 (RS): *(p1, k1, p1); rep from * to last 3 sts, (p1, k1, p1).

Work 11 further rows in patt.
Change to C leaving a tail approx 8in (20cm) long.
Work 3 rows g-st.
Break off C leaving a tail approx 8in (20cm) long for fringe.
Join in B and work 9 rows in patt.
Change to C leaving a tail as before.
Work 3 rows g-st.

Break off C leaving a tail as before.
Join in A and work 13 rows in patt.
Change to C leaving a tail as before.
Work 3 rows g-st.
Cast off k-wise leaving a tail approx 8in (20cm) long.

Lining (optional)

Using 5mm needles and A cast on 27 sts and work (22 rows g-st in A, then 22 rows g-st in B) twice.
Cast off loosely k-wise.

Making up

Darn in ends of yarns A and B. Cover work with a damp cloth and dry flat to set the stitches. Sew in the lining (if used) leaving a narrow border all around.

This design by Bernice Watkins uses only basic crochet stitches to produce a complex, textured fabric. Best of all, there's no need to sew in the ends as they form the fringe.

Fringe folk

Materials

Any 4-ply yarn (2 strands used tog) or any DK yarn
Small amount of tan, chocolate, rust, peach and cream
A 4mm crochet hook
2 hook-and-eye fastenings
Darning needle
Sewing needle and thread

Tension

Not critical as rows are added until the piece is long enough to fit round the coffee jug

Method

This cozy is crocheted sideways in treble and double crochet, working from R to L from RS through front and back loops, changing colours on every row.

Cozy

Using 4mm hook and tan, make 31ch.
Foundation row 1 (RS): Miss 1ch (t-ch), dc into each ch to end (30 sts).
Foundation row 2 (WS): 1ch, dc through front loops only to end.

Fasten off leaving a 3in (7.5cm) tail. Working all subsequent rows with RS facing and following colour sequence work in pattern until piece measures 11¾in (30cm). The repeating sequence for the pattern is shown in chocolate, rust, peach, cream and tan – or use any combination of colours.

Pattern

Row 1: Join yarn leaving an end for the fringe. 1ch (t-ch), * (5tr into front loops of the next 5dc of foundation row 1; 5dc into back loops of the next 5dc of foundation row 2), rep from * to end. Fasten off leaving a 3in (7.5cm) tail.

Row 2: Join yarn and make1ch (t-ch), * (5dc into back loops of the next 5tr of patt row 1; 5tr into front loops of the next 5dc of foundation row 2), rep from * to end.
Fasten off leaving a 3in (7.5cm) tail.
Row 3: Join yarn, 1ch (t-ch), * (5tr into front loops of the next 5tr of the second-to-last row; 5dc into back loops of the next 5tr of last row), rep from * to end.
Fasten off leaving a 3in (7.5cm) tail.
Row 4: Join yarn and make1ch (t-ch), * (5dc into back loops of the next 5tr of last row; 5tr into front loops of the next 5tr of second-to-last row), rep from * to end.
Fasten off leaving a 3in (7.5cm) tail.
Rep rows 3–4 for patt, keeping colour sequence correct (see patt notes).

Making up

Attach hook-and-eye fastenings. Trim fringe ends to standard length, or sew in yarn ends if you do not want a fringe.

> ### Tip
> This design is ideal for using up oddments as each row needs only about 2yds (2m) of yarn.

This design by Jemma Langworthy continues a tradition that dates back more than 130 years, for Cockneys from the east end of London to decorate their clothes with mother-of-pearl buttons sewn in intricate patterns.

Pearly queen

Materials

Standard chunky wool or wool-mix yarn

1 x 50g ball black

A pair of 5mm (US8:UK6) needles

3 press fasteners

Selection of small buttons (mother-of-pearl if possible)

3 x large matching buttons

Sewing needle and black thread

Tension

16 sts to 4in (10cm) in width over moss stitch using 5mm needles

Use larger or smaller needles if necessary to obtain correct tension

Special techniques

Moss stitch (m-st)

Method

The cozy is worked sideways in moss stitch, making fastening tabs just before casting off.

Cozy

Cast on 29 sts and work in m-st until cozy is long enough to reach round coffee jug.

Tabs

Next row: * K5, turn.
Work 4 rows in m-st over these 5 sts.
Next row: Work 2 sts tog, m-st 3, work 2 sts tog.
Work 1 row in m-st.
Next row: K1, k2tog, psso.
Fasten off.

Rejoin yarn to rem sts and cast off 7 sts.*
Next row: Work from * to *.
Rejoin yarn to rem sts and cast off 7 sts.
Work last tab on rem 5 sts.
Fasten off.

Making up

Sew in ends of yarn. Using sewing thread, attach press studs to back of tabs and cover, lining up carefully. Attach 3 large matching buttons to front of tabs. Arrange smaller buttons on cover, either randomly or forming patterns as is traditional. Sew in place.

An appropriate theme of dainty coffee cups worked in fairisle is the choice for this design by Elizabeth Stringer. The ingenious 'steam' effect is added afterwards.

Cappuccino

Materials

Sirdar Luxury Soft Cotton DK 100% natural cotton (104yds/95m per 50g ball)

1 x 50g ball in 672 Chocolate (A)

1 x 50g ball in 660 Calico (B)

1 x 50g ball in 656 Walnut (C)

A pair of 4mm (US6:UK8) needles

Sewing needle and coordinating thread

Darning needle

Felt for backing

Tension

22 sts and 28 rows to 4in (10cm) over st st using 4mm needles

Use larger or smaller needles to achieve correct tension

Special techniques

Fairisle

Method

This cozy is knitted from bottom to top with a moss stitch border. Simple ties made from lengths of yarn are attached to the corners.

Cozy

Using B, cast on 65 sts.

Rows 1–3: (k1, p1) to end.

Row 4: (k1, p1, k1) in B, join in A and p to last 3 sts, join in B and (k1, p1, k1).

Row 5: (k1, p1, k1) in B, k to last 3 sts in A, (k1, p1, k1) in B.

Row 6: (k1, p1, k1) in B, p to end in A, (k1, p1, k1) in B.

Row 7: As row 5.

Row 8: As row 6.

Row 9 (RS): Using B, (k1, p1, k1); k5 in A; foll chart for left cup; k5 in A, foll chart for right cup; k5 in A, (k1, p1, k1) in B.

Row 10 (RS): Using B, (k1, p1, k1); p5 in A, foll chart for right cup; p5 in A, foll chart for left cup; p5 in A, (k1, p1, k1) in B.

Rep rows 9–10 until chart is complete (26 rows), then rep rows 5–6 eight times (42 rows).

Row 42: As row 5.

Rows 43–46: (k1, p1, k1) to end in B.

Embroidered steam*

For running stitches, cut 8 lengths of B and 4 lengths of C, each 12in (30cm) long. Thread 2 lengths of C on to a darning needle. Darn from back to front at C1, from front to back at C2, bring back to front at C3 and front to back again at C4.

Thread 2 lengths of B on to a darning needle. Darn from back to front at B1, then from front to back at B2; from back to front at B3 and then from front to back at B4; from back to front at B5, then from front to back at B6; from back to front at B7, then from front to back at B8.

Tacking

Tease 2 strands from another 12in (30cm) length of B. Using 2 strands together, tack as shown on the chart to 'shape' the smoke. Repeat for the other cup.

Making up

Cut felt backing to fit and attach to cover using a sewing needle and coordinating thread. Darn in ends if necessary.

Ties

Cut 4 x 8in (20cm) strands of each colour yarn and group into 4 sets of 3, a single colour in each set. Thread the strands through the moss stitch border at the side, at top left, top right, bottom left and bottom right. Knot securely so there is an equal length on both sides of the fabric, trimming if necessary.

Note

The steam is worked in Swiss darning after the cozy is knitted.

Cappuccino steam chart *22 sts x 26 rows*

Each square = 1 st and 1 row
Read RS rows from R to L and WS rows from L to R

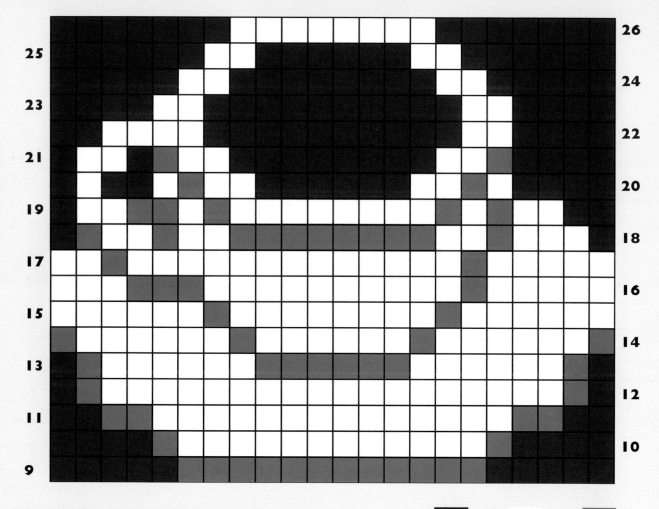

Cappuccino left cup chart *22 sts x 26 rows*

Each square = I st and I row

Read RS rows from R to L and WS rows from L to R

A  B C

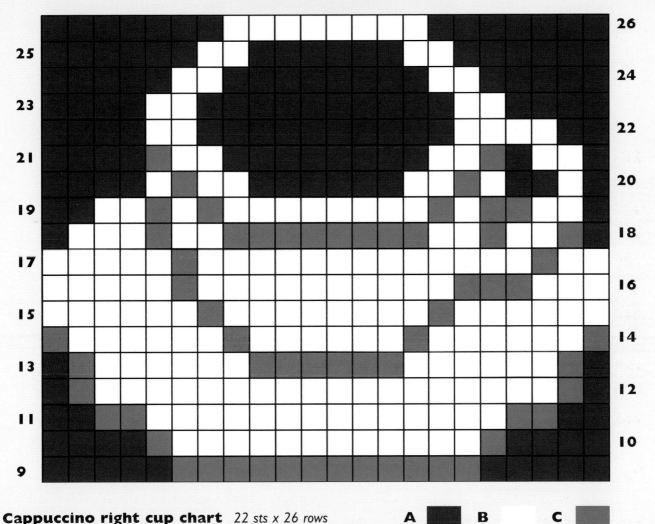

Cappuccino right cup chart *22 sts x 26 rows*

Each square = 1 st and 1 row

Read RS rows from R to L and WS rows from L to R

A ■ B □ C ▦

This lovely textured design by Helen Betts is worked sideways, using a crisp mercerized cotton yarn and a ridge pattern that looks impressive but is very easy to work.

Textured stripe

Materials

Garnstudio Muskat (109yds/100m per 50g ball)

1 x 50g ball in 19 Light Grey (M)

1 x 50g ball in 12 Red (C)

A pair of 4.5mm (US7:UK7) needles

4 x buttons

Tension

23 sts and 32 rows to 4in (10cm) measured over garter stitch using 4.5mm needles

Use larger or smaller needles if necessary to obtain correct tension

Special techniques

Garter stitch (g-st)

Method

This highly-textured cozy is knitted sideways in garter stitch with contrasting stocking stitch 'ridges' in stocking stitch. Button loops are formed within the cast-off.

Cozy

Using 4.5mm needles and M, cast on 40 sts and work 9 rows in g-st.
*Place first and last 4 sts on stitch holders.
Join in C and work 8 rows st st on centre 32 sts only.
Change to M and work in g-st on all 40 sts.

Next row: K4, work 32 sts by knitting into each st along with its corresponding st from the first C row (to close gap and form ridge), k4. Using M, work a further 3 rows in g-st *. Rep from * to * 20 times (21 ridges in total).
Work 2 more g-st rows in M.

Button loop cast-off row: Cast off 4, make 4 ch (crochet-style, with tips of needles) for button loop, cast off 11, make 4 ch, cast off 10, make 4 ch, cast off 11, make 4 ch, cast off rem 4 sts.
Note: the number of ch sts per loop may need adjustment to accommodate the size of buttons chosen.

Making up

Sew in ends. The yarn does not bind easily, so weave ends in thoroughly to make sure stitches do not come undone. Sew on buttons.

Thick yarn and large needles are used for this quickly-worked design
by Jacqui Lewington. It fastens with duffel coat-style toggles that
complement the chunky yarn.

Freshly roasted

Materials

Debbie Bliss Como superchunky (42m/46yds per 100g ball)

2 x 50g balls in 16 Beige

A pair of 10mm (US15:UK000) needles

A 10mm (USN/P-15:UK000) crochet hook

3 x wooden toggles

Large darning needle

Tension

12.5 sts and 12 rows to 4in (10cm) over patt using
10mm needles

Use larger or smaller needles to obtain correct tension.

Special techniques

Yarn forward (yf): Bring yarn to front of work

Yarn back (yb): Take yarn to back of work

Method

The 'woven' pattern effect is formed by slipping stitches and carrying the yarn across, making a very thick fabric.

Cozy

Using 10mm needles cast on 41 sts.

Foundation row: Purl.

Now work in pattern as folls:

Pattern

K2 (sl, kl) to last st, kl

Row 2: Pl (kl, yf, sl, yb) to last 2 sts, kl, pl.

Row 3: Kl (sl, kl) to end.

Row 4: Pl (sl, pl) to end.

Row 5: Kl, yf, sl, ytb, sl, (yf, s3, ytb, sl) to last 2 sts, yf, sll, yb, kl.

Row 6: Pl, yb, sl, yf, sl, (yb, s3, yf, sl) to last 2 sts, yb, sll, yf, pl.

Row 7: As row 1.

Row 8: As row 2.

Row 9: As row 3.

Row 10: As row 4.

Row 11: Kl (yf, sl3, yb, sl) to last 4 sts, yf, s3, yb, kl.

Row 12: Pl (yb, sl3, yf, sl) to last 4 sts, yb, s3, yf, pl.

These 12 rows form the pattern.

Repeat until 44 rows in total have been worked, excluding the foundation row. Cast off.

Making up

Attach the toggles to the cozy.

Make crochet loops and sew to the opposite side to fasten toggles.

This cozy by Ally Howard is made from pure merino wool, felted for extra thickness. Easy blanket stitch edging is also used to finish off hearts cut from felted knitted fabric.

Heartfelt

Materials

Elle Merino Solids (77yds/70m per 50g ball)

1 x 50g ball in 169 Cherry Red

Oddment of any wool yarn suitable for felting in complementary shade

Oddment of black chunky yarn for edging and button loops

A pair of 7mm (US10.5:UK2) needles

A 5mm (USH/8:UK6) crochet hook

3 x contrasting buttons

Sharp large-eyed needle

Tension

14 sts and 24 rows to 4in (10cm) over g-st using 7mm needles

Use larger or smaller needles to achieve correct tension

Special techniques

Garter stitch (g-st)

Blanket stitch

Felting (see pattern instructions)

Method

The cover is worked big because the yarn shrinks by at least a third during the felting process.

Cozy

Cast on 52 sts and work in g-st until work measures 9in (23cm).
Cast off.

Fabric for hearts

Using oddment of DK, cast on 20 sts and work in g-st until work measures 5in (12.5cm).
Cast off.

Felting

Place the small piece of knitting and the main cover in separate washing bags. Place in the drum of a washing machine with a small amount of detergent. Add a thick towel to provide the friction necessary for the felting process to take place. Set machine temperature to 40°C and run though a full cycle. Remove work from machine and check that it has felted sufficiently. If not, repeat the process. Pull work to correct shape and measurements of 11¾in x 6¾in (30cm x 17cm) and allow to dry completely.

Tip

If substituting yarn, remember that yarns containing acrylic, or wool yarn treated to be 'superwash' will not felt.

Making up

Press pieces lightly. Work blanket stitch round edge of cover, making 3 chain loops (with crochet hook) at top, centre and lower edge of the cover. Sew on buttons to correspond with loops. Cut heart shapes from small piece of knitted fabric, angling heart templates diagonally. Blanket stitch hearts to front of cover, positioning them at an angle.

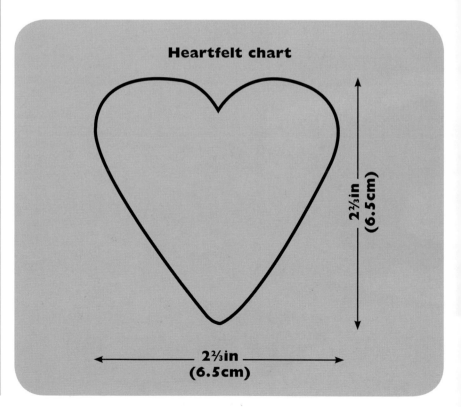

Heartfelt chart

2⅔in (6.5cm)

2⅔in (6.5cm)

The flavour of the Scottish Highlands is the inspiration for this colourful cozy by Pat Strong. Like its biscuity namesake, it's the perfect companion for a cup of coffee.

Shortbread crunch

Materials

Rowan Pure Wool DK (136yds/125m per 50g ball)

1 x 50g ball in 036 Kiss (red)

1 x 50g ball in 021 Glade (green)

1 x 50g ball in 013 Enamel (cream)

A pair of 4mm (US6:UK8) needles

48in (120cm) x ½in (1cm) tartan ribbon, cut into 6 equal lengths

Sewing needle and coordinating thread

Darning needle

Tension

22 sts x 30 rows to 4in (10cm) over st st using 4mm needles
Use larger or smaller needles to achieve correct tension.

Special techniques

Moss stitch (m-st)

Fairisle

Method

The back (lining) is knitted in moss stitch in red, and the front (outer) piece is made following the fairisle chart, with a 2-st/2row moss stitch border. Finally, three pairs of tartan ribbon are sewn on as ties.

Lining

Using red, cast on 65 sts.
Work 50 rows in m-st.
Cast off.

Front

Using cream, cast on 66 sts.
Follow chart, working border in m-st and the rest in st st fairisle.
Cast off using cream.

Making up

Press front piece only, avoiding the moss stitch areas. Using a sewing needle, attach the lengths of ribbon to give 3 sets of ties. Using a darning needle and with wrong sides together, join front to back.

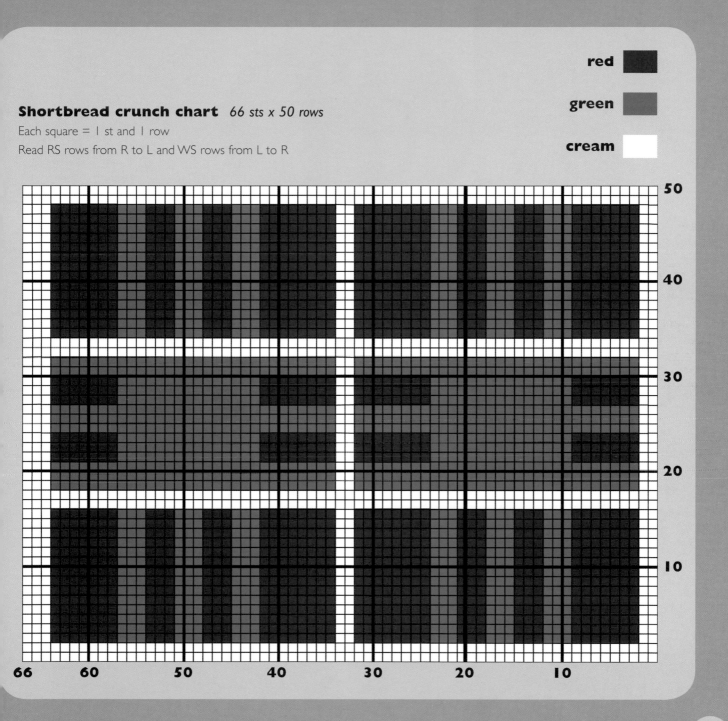

Shortbread crunch chart *66 sts x 50 rows*

Each square = 1 st and 1 row

Read RS rows from R to L and WS rows from L to R

red
green
cream

Textured contrast yarn, lace panels and a lacy border combine
to make this design by Janine Dempster a real visual delight.
Toggles and crochet loops are used to fasten it.

Secret garden

Materials

Debbie Bliss Donegal Aran Tweed (96yds/88m per 50g ball)
1 x 50g ball in 281122 Dark Green (M)
Adriafil Retro Trends (30yds/27.5m per 50g ball)
1 x 50g ball in 062 5572 (C)
A pair of 4mm (US6:UK8) needles
A pair of 5mm (US8:UK6) needles
A 4mm (USG/6:UK8) crochet hook
3 x wooden toggles
Darning needle

Tension

18 sts and 30 rows to 4in (10cm) over patt using
4mm needles
Use larger or smaller needles to achieve correct tension

Method

The main piece is knitted from bottom to top, with garter stitch borders and short rows of textured contrast yarn inserted near the beginning and end. The centre pattern is diagonal lace and the lacy border is knitted sideways and sewn on afterwards.

Cozy

Using 5mm needles and M, cast on 49 sts.

Row 1 (RS): P3, k43, p3.
Row 2 (WS): Purl.
Row 3: As row 1.
Row 4: Purl.
Row 5: As row 1.

Now follow the instructions and work the two short rows before returning to the pattern:

Short rows

Row A (WS): Slip first 3 sts on to right needle, join in C and p43, turn (leaving last 3 sts unworked).
Row B (RS): Still using C, k43, sl last 3 sts on to right needle. Break off C and cont patt from row 6:
Row 6: Purl.
Row 7: As row 1.
Row 8: Purl.
Row 9: As row 1.
Row 10: Purl.
Now work in lace patt:

Row 11 (RS): P3, k1, (yo, sl1, k2, psso) to last 3 sts, p3.
Row 12: Purl.
Row 13: P3, k2 (yo, sl1, k2, psso) to last 5 sts, (yo sl1, k1, psso), p3.
Row 14: Purl.
Row 15: P3, k3, (yo, sl1, k2, psso) to last 4 sts, k1, p3.
Row 16: Purl.
Rows 11–16 form lace patt. Rep these rows twice, ending with a purl row.
Row 29: P3, k43, p3.
Row 29: Purl.
Row 30: P3, k43, p3.
Next: Work short rows A and B again. Cast off.

Lacy trim

Using 4mm needles and M, cast on 11 sts.
Next row: (WS) Purl.
Row 1 (RS): K3, yo, k2tog, k1, sl1, k1, psso, turn, cast on 4, turn, k2tog, k1 (13 sts).
Row 2: K10, yf, k2tog, k1.

Row 3: K3, yo, k2tog, sl1, k1, psso (yo, k1) 4 times, yo, k2tog (16 sts).
Row 4: K13, yo, k2tog, k1.
Row 5: K3, yo, k2tog, sl1, k1, psso (yo, k1) twice, yo, sl1, k2tog, psso, (yo, k1) twice, yo, k2tog (18 sts).
Row 6: K15, yo, k2tog, k1.
Row 7: k3, yo, k2tog, k11, k2tog (17 sts).
Row 8: Cast off 6, k7, yo, k2tog, k1 (11 sts).
Rep these 8 rows 7 yimes,
Cast off k-wise.

Making up

Lay work face down on ironing board. Cover with a damp cloth and press gently on a low setting, avoiding contast yarn (to keep its bulk and shape). Sew in ends using a darning needle.

With work right side up, lay trim along bottom of work and pin in place. Using M, pick up 1 st from main piece and 1 st from edge of trim, and sew together in a loop fashion, taking care not to pull too tight. This will give a 3D effect to the trim.

Attach wooden toggles. Crochet 3 chains for loops and sew on opposite edge to correspond with toggles.

An ingenious use of sequined gift wrap ribbon gives this simple design by Anita Ursula Nycs extra sparkle. If you make this as a gift, why not use the same ribbon to wrap it?

Party time

Materials

Any acrylic DK yarn in dusky pink
A pair of 5mm (UK6:US8) needles
4mm (UK8:USG/6) crochet hook
A piece of purple fabric 7 x 12in (18 x 31cm)
6 x 6¾in (17cm) lengths of iridescent gift wrap ribbon
3 x buttons
Sewing needle and coordinating thread
Darning needle

Tension

19.5 sts and 27 rows to 4in (10cm) over patt using 5mm needles
Use larger or smaller needles to achieve correct tension

Method

The main part is worked in 4 x 4 rib with added double crochet edging and button loops.

Cozy

Usng 5mm needles, cast on 52 sts.

Row 1: K4, (p4, k4) to end.

Row 2: P4, (k4, p4) to end.

Rep these 2 rows until work measures 6¾in (17cm)

Cast off.

Edging

Using the 4mm crochet hook, work 4 rows dc along each short edge of cozy. Make 3 chains for button loops and sew on. Attach buttons to correspond with loops. Darn in any loose ends.

Making up

'Couch' the gift wrap ribbon vertically along the 4-stitch purled columns and catch in place using sewing needle and coordinating thread.

Lining

Sew lining to the knitted piece, allowing ¼in (0.5cm) for turnover.

This cheerful design by Frankie Brown is really easy to make, and every little duck is given its own characteristics and cheeky personality.

Ducks on parade

Materials

Debbie Bliss Cashmerino DK (110m/125yds per 50g ball)

1 x 50g ball in 18009 Blue

Patons Fairytale Colour 4 Me DK (90m/98yds per 50g ball)

Small amount in 4960 Yellow

Oddment of any DK yarn in orange

Black seed beads for eyes

A pair of 3.25mm (UK10:US3) needles

4 x ½in (1.5cm) buttons

Sewing needle and black thread

Darning needle

Tension

25 sts and 35 rows to 4in (10cm) over st st using 3.25mm needles

Use larger or smaller needles to achieve correct tension.

Special techniques

Reverse stocking stitch (rev st st): use reverse of stocking stitch as the right side

Garter stitch (g-st)

Method

The main piece is worked first, beginning and ending with reverse stocking stitch with the main panel in stocking stitch. Stitches are picked up and worked in garter stitch for the button bands and buttonhole bands.

Cozy

Using blue, cast on 70 sts.

Beg with a p row, work 4 rows in rev st st.

Beg with a k row, work 55 rows in st st.

For the top edge begin with a k row and work 4 rows in rev st st.

Cast off k-wise.

Button bands

With RS facing pick up and k 40 sts along one side. The top and bottom of the sides should be allowed to curl naturally and worked as one layer.

Working on the first 6 sts only, work 6 rows g-st and cast off.

Rejoin yarn and cast off the next 6 sts.

Working on the next 16 sts, work 6 rows g-st and cast off.

Rejoin yarn and cast off the next 6 sts.

Working on the last 6 sts, work 6 rows g-st and cast off.

Buttonhole bands

With RS facing, pick up and k 40 sts along the other side, allowing the top and bottom to curl as before.

Working on the first 6 sts only, work 2 rows g-st.

Next row: K2, cast off 2 sts, k2.

Next row: K2, cast on 2 sts, k2.

Work 2 more rows in g-st and cast off. Rejoin yarn and cast off the next 6 sts. Working on the next 16 sts, work 2 rows g-st.

Next row: K3, cast off 2 sts, k6, cast off 2 sts, k3.

Next row: K3, cast on 2 sts, k6, cast on 2 sts, k3.

Work 2 more rows in g-st and cast off. Rejoin yarn and cast off the next 6 sts. On the last 6 sts only, work 2 rows g-st.

Next row: K2, cast off 2 sts, k2.

Next row: K2, cast on 2 sts, k2.

Work 2 more rows in g-st and cast off.

Making up

Sew the 4 buttons to the button bands to correspond with the buttonholes.

Ducks (make 6)

Using yellow, cast on 10 sts.

Row 1: Purl.
Row 2: K1, m1, k8, m1, k1.
Row 3: Purl.
Row 4: K1, m1, k to end.
Row 5: Purl.
Row 6: As row 4.
Row 7: P2tog tbl, p to end.
Row 8: As row 4.
Row 9: As row 7.
Row 10: K2, k2tog, turn.
Row 11: Sl1 p-wise, p2tog, psso, then fasten off. Rejoin yarn and cast off 5 sts, k to end (4 sts).
Row 12: Purl.
Row 13: K1, m1, k2, m1, k1.
Row 14: Purl.
Row 15: K5, m1, k1.
Row 16: Purl.
Row 17: K2tog, k to end.
Row 18: P2tog tbl, p to end.
Cast off.

Beaks (make 6)

Using orange, cast on 1 st and k into the front and back of this st (2 sts). K 1 row and cast off.

Wings (make 6)

Using yellow, cast on 2 sts.

Row 1: Purl.
Row 2: K1, m1, k1.
Row 3: Purl.
Row 4: K1, m1, k2.
Row 5: Purl.
Row 6: Knit.
Row 7: Purl.
Row 8: K2tog, k2.
Row 9: Sl1 p-wise, p2tog, psso and fasten off.

Assembling the ducks

Sew the wing to the duck with the cast-off point facing forwards. Attach the beak to the side of the head for a sideways facing duck, or to the front of the head if you want the duck to face you. Using black sewing thread, sew on black seed bead for the eyes: one for a side-facing duck and two for a forward-facing duck.

Arrange the ducks on the cozy in two rows of three and sew firmly in place. Sew in any loose ends.

Ring the changes with this intarsia design by Charlotte Walford.
It has two sides, and one is a negative image of the other,
so it's completely reversible.

Morning coffee

Materials

Patons Diploma Gold 4-ply (201yds/184m per 50g ball)

1 x 50g ball 4218 Chocolate

1 x 50g ball 4281 White

A pair of 3mm (US2–3:UK11) needles

A spare 3mm needle (for 3-needle cast-off)

Oddments of waste yarn to use as stitch holders

6 x yarn bobbins or small pieces of card

3 x ½in (1.3cm) snap fasteners

Tension

28 stitches and 36 rows to 10cm (4in) measured over st st
using 3mm needles

Use larger or smaller needles if necessary to achieve the
correct tension.

Special techniques

Intarsia

3-needle cast-off (see pattern instructions)

Moss stitch (m-st)

Method

Motifs are worked using the intarsia method in stocking stitch, but stranding the yarn across back of work between pot and spout and pot and handle. Side 1 is knitted first, then sts are picked up from the cast-on edge to work side 2. The tops of the 2 sides are joined using a 3-needle cast off. Upper and lower tabs are worked as part of the main fabric; centre tabs are made separately.

Preparing the yarn

Before starting chart for side 1, wind white yarn on 2 separate bobbins for pots, and chocolate on 3 bobbins for background. For side 2, wind chocolate on 2 bobbins for pots, and white on 3 bobbins for background.

Side 1

Cast on 98 sts in white. *
Rows 1–5: Work in m-st.
Row 6: Cont in m-st, cast off 11 sts in patt at beg of next 2 rows (76 sts).

Intarsia pattern

Change to chocolate. Beg with row 1 of chart and a k row, work background in chocolate and pots in white.
Foll chart for 50 rows.

Upper border and tabs

Change to white and k 1 row.
Turn and cast on 11 sts (87 sts).
Next row: (k1, p1) to last st, k1.
Turn and cast on 11 sts (98 sts).
Next row: Still using white, work 5 rows m-st.
Place sts on waste yarn, leaving an end approx 138in (350cm). Sew in ends.*.

Side 2

Lower border and tabs

With RS of side 1 facing, and using chocolate, pick up 98 sts along cast-on edge (one for each st).
Work as side 1 from * to *, but reversing colours.

Embroidering the dots

Using a cool iron, press both sides lightly on the WS under a clean dry cloth. Embroider dots using French knots (see chart for placement), in chocolate for the knots on side 1, and white for the knots on side 2. Take care not to pucker the fabric during this step, as the cosy must be able to stretch to grip the cafetière. Darn in yarn ends carefully along colour joins.

Three needle cast-off

Transfer sts from the top edge of side 1 from waste yarn to one needle, and sts from the top edge of side 2 to another needle.
Place right sides of work together. Using a third needle pick up the first st from side 1 and the first st from side 2 and k2tog. Rep along row, knitting tog one st from each side, and casting them off in the normal way as you go. Fasten off and sew in ends. Turn the cozy right side out.
Sew snap fasteners to top and bottom tabs to fasten cozy.

Join sides

With RS facing and using white, pick up 40 sts along left edge of side 1.
Work 7 rows in m st but do not cast off. Place sts on a spare needle ready to work the three-needle cast off later. Rep for the right edge of side 2, using chocolate. Carefully turn the cozy inside out. Right sides facing, work the two sets of sts tog using the three-needle cast off so the cast-off edge is on the inside of the cozy. Turn the cozy right side out and join the small seams around the tabs using mattress stitch. Sew in all ends before the next step. Join the rem side seam as above; but instead of leaving the sts on a holder, cast off each set of sts individually. Join the two sides using mattress stitch.

Morning coffee chart *36 sts x 34 rows*

Each square = 1 st and 1 row

Begin at the left side of chart

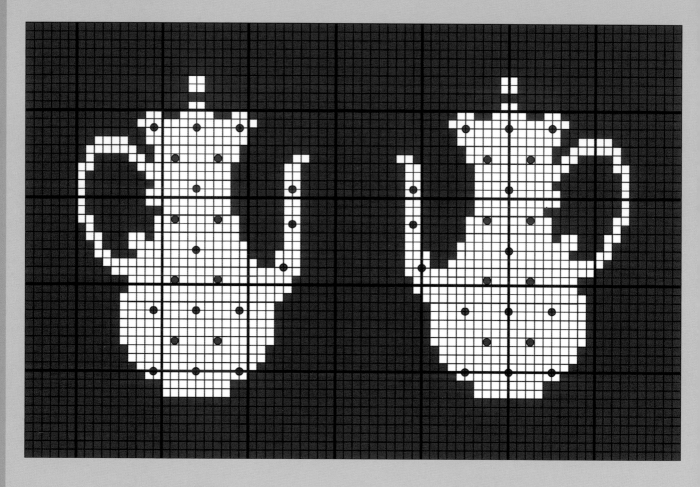

Chocolate

Cream

Note: reverse colours for second side

Carefully and securely darn the rem yarn ends into the cozy, and join rem small seams using mattress stitch. Press the borders and tabs of the cozy again lightly under a clean dry cloth so they lie straight. Take care not to flatten the moss stitch too much.

Centre tabs
(make one in white and one in chocolate)

First tab
Using white cast on 7 sts and work 7 rows in m-st.
Cast off in m-st.

Second tab
Work another tab as given above, using chocolate yarn instead of white.

Making up
Using mattress stitch, attach the white tab to the centre of the RH edge of side 1, and the chocolate tab to the centre of the RH edge of side 2. Attach one half of the snap fastener to the first tab, and the other half to the second tab.

This pretty cover by Bernice Watkins in an easy honeycomb rib pattern is really fast to work, thanks to thick yarn, big needles and no-fuss hook-and-eye dot fastenings.

Sky blue

Materials

Any bulky yarn
1 x 50g ball in sky blue
A pair of 8mm (US11:UK0) needles
3 x ¾in (2cm) hook and eye tape dots
Darning needle

Tension

Not critical as fabric is quite stretchy.

Special techniques

Double brioche pattern (see instructions)

Method

The cozy is knitted from bottom to top in a honeycomb-style stitch, with bright red hook-and-eye tape dots added for easy fastening.

Cozy

Using 8mm needles cast on 30 sts. Keeping the first and last st of each row in m-st, work the rem 28 centre sts in double brioche patt until piece measures 6¾in (17cm).

Double brioche pattern

Foundation row: * yf, sl1 p-wise (leaving yarn at front to create a yo before next st), k1, rep from * to end.

Row 1: Purl all sts, slipping each yo from previous row p-wise.

Row 2: * k tog (yo plus next st), yf, sl1 p-wise (leaving yarn at front to create a yo before next st), rep from * to end.

Row 3: As row 1.

Row 4: * yf, sl1 p-wise, (leaving yarn at front to create a yo before next st), k2tog (yo plus next st), rep from * to end of row

The last four rows form patt. Rep to length required.

Cast off.

Making up

Fix the tape dots 1in (2.5cm) from top and bottom and one in the middle. The work should overlap by approx 1in (2.5cm).

Tip

The cozy can be fastened with large press-studs if preferred.

This scrumptious design by Emma Rowlstone is made in shades to match your favourite cup of coffee, and the felted lining adds extra warmth.

Mocha choca latte

Materials

Rowan Cocoon (126yds/115m per 50g ball)

1 × 50g ball 00801 Polar

1 × 50g ball 00809 Crag

A pair of 7mm (US10.5:UK2) needles

3 × buttons

Sewing thread and needle

Tension

12.5 sts and 16 rows to 4cm (10cm) over st st using 7mm needles

Use larger or smaller needles to obtain correct tension

Special techniques

Cable cast-on

Garter stitch

Method

The lining of this cozy is made first and felted. The textured outer piece is worked in a single piece from lower edge to top and the two layers are joined, then a buttonband is added.

Lining

Using 7mm needles, cast on 41 sts. Work in st st until piece measures 7¾in (19cm). Cast off and weave in ends. Run through a full cycle in the washing machine at 40°C with some other garments so that it felts. If more felting is necessary felt again, or try placing in a tumble dryer for 5-minute periods until correct size is achieved. While damp, pin out to approx 6 x 11in (15 x 28cm), pulling the piece into shape quite firmly if necessary. Leave pinned out until completely dry.

Textured outer layer

Using cable cast-on technique and 7mm needles, cast on 42 sts.
Work 2 rows g-st, then work in pattern as folls:
Row 1: (RS) Sl1 k-wise, k2, purl to last 3 sts, k2, k1 tbl.
Row 2: Sl1 k-wise, k2, * (k1, p1, k1) into next st, p3tog: rep from * to last 3 sts, k2, k1 tbl.
Row 3: As row 1.
Row 4: Sl1 k-wise, k2, *p3tog, (k1, p1, k1) into next st: rep from * to last 3 sts, k2, k1 tbl.
Rep until piece measures 6in (15cm) ending with a p row.
K 1 row, then cast off k-wise.
Weave in ends and block.

Making up

Place outer layer RS down. Place inner, felted layer face down (purl side up) on the outer layer. Pin the two layers together, then sew around the edge of the felted layer using small but firm stitches.

With RS facing and cast-off edge at the top, attach buttons to the left edge, placing top and bottom buttons ¾in (2cm) from edge and the third button midway between.

Button band

With RS facing, pick up 16 sts.
Row 1: K3, yo, k5, yo, k5, yo, k3.
Row 2: Cast off k-wise.
Weave in ends.

Star-shaped sequins twinkle on a midnight blue background on Charmaine Fletcher's night-time knit that is perfect for convivial dinner parties. The basket weave texture adds interest.

Night sky

Materials

Palette Collection DK (348yds/320m per 100g ball)

1 x 100g ball in Navy

A pair of 3mm (US3:UK11) needles

A pair of 4mm (US6:UK8:) needles

A pair of 2.5mm (US1:UK13:) double-pointed needles

A 3mm (USC2-D/3:UK11) crochet hook

6¾in x 11¾in (17cm x 30cm) piece of royal blue or navy felt

3 x ¼in (1cm) navy star-shaped buttons

11 x silver star-shaped sequins

Sewing needle and 'invisible' sewing thread

Tapestry needle and dressmaker's pins

Tension

23 sts and 29 rows to 4in (10cm) over st st using 4mm needles

Use larger or smaller needles to obtain correct tension

Special techniques

Thumb method cast-on

Moss stitch (m-st)

Making an I-cord

Method

The cozy is knitted in one piece from bottom to top in stocking stitch and a basket-weave pattern with a moss stitch border.

Cozy

Using 4mm needles and the thumb method, cast on 65 sts.

Lower border

Work 5 rows in m-st.
Now work basket-weave section with m-st edging.

Basket-weave pattern

Row 1 (RS): * m-st 5, (k5, p5) to last 5 sts, m-st 5.
Row 2: M-st 5, (p5, k5) to last 5 sts, m-st 5.
Row 3: As row 1.
Row 4: As row 2.
Row 5: As row 1.
Row 6: As row 2.
Row 7: As row 1.
Row 8 (WS): M-st 5, (k5, p5) to last 5 sts, m-st 5.
Row 9: M-st 5, (p5, k5) to last 5 sts, m-st 5.
Row 10: As row 8.
Row 11: As row 9.
Row 12: As row 8.
Row 13: As row 9.
Row 14: As row 8.

Rep from * once.
Work st st section with m-st edging:
Row 1: M-st 5 sts, work in st st to last 5 sts, m-st 5 sts.
Rows 2–17: As last row.
Work 5 rows in m-st for upper border.
Change to 3mm needles and cast off leaving a tail 24in (60cm) long. Using running stitch, draw this tail along the cast off edge, to create a firmer edge.

Button loops (make 3)

Using 2.5mm double-pointed needles make an i-cord 3¼in (8cm) long. Cast off, leaving long tails for sewing.

Alternative button loops

Using a 3mm hook make 22 ch sts. Fasten off.

Making up

Sew button loops to side of work, between moss stitch side border and main pattern. Attach buttons to opposite side to correspond with buttons. Attach the sequins at intervals along the stocking stitch section.

Lining

Pin the felt to the back of the knitted piece, stretching if necessary, and sew into place.

Tiny cables add a classic twist to this design by Phyllis Ely.
The unusual baby cable is worked across only three stitches,
so the knitted fabric does not pull in too tightly.

Cable classic

Materials

Sirdar Click chunky (70yds/75m per 50g ball)

1 x 50g ball in 150 Greenapple

A pair of 5mm (US8:UK6) needles

A pair of 5.5mm (US9:UK5) needles

Cable needle

3 x ¾in (2cm) buttons

Tension

Not critical, as the cable pattern is very stretchy

Special techniques

Single rib

T3L: twist 3 sts left (slip next st on to cable needle and bring
to front of work, k2, then k st from cable needle)

Method

The cozy is worked in one piece from bottom to top, beginning and ending with a traditional 1x1 rib. A 2-st moss stitch border on either side forms the button bands.

Cozy

Using 5mm needles cast on 51 sts and work 2 rows 1x1 rib.

Next row (buttonhole row): Rib 2, yf, k2tog, rib to end.

Next row: Work in rib, inc 1 st at each end of row (53 sts).

Change to 5.5mm needles and work in patt as folls:

Cable pattern

Row 1: K3, (p2, k3, p2, k1) to last 2 sts, k2.

Row 2 (and all even rows): K2, p1, (k2, p3, k2, p1) 2 sts, k2.

Row 3: K3, (p2, T3L, p2, k1) to last 2 sts, k2.

Row 4: As row 2.

Rows 5–16: Rep rows 1–4, 3 times.

Next row (buttonhole row): K2, yf, p2tog, work in patt to end.

Work in patt until work measures 6¼in (15.5cm), ending on a WS row.

Next row (buttonhole): Rib 2, yf, p2tog, rib to end.

Next row: Work in rib, dec 1 st at each end of row (51 sts).

Change to 5mm needles and work 2 more rows in 1x1 rib.

Cast off in rib.

Making up

Do not press. Sew in ends of yarn. Attach buttons to correspond with buttonholes.

> ### Tip
> *Don't worry if the work looks too narrow: it will stretch widthways to fit!*

This jolly design in easy double crochet by Anita Ursula Nycs uses cheerful rainbow-bright colours, and is also a brilliant way to use up tiny scraps of yarn.

Checks and stripes

Materials

Any DK yarn in purple

Oddments of DK in red, light blue, mid-blue, yellow and green

A 4mm (USG/6:UK8) crochet hook

A piece of purple fabric 7in × 12in (18cm × 31cm)

3 × purple buttons

Darning needle

Sewing needle and thread

Tension

17 sts and 21 rows approx to 4in (10cm) over double crochet using 4mm hook

Use larger or smaller hook to achieve correct tension

Method

The main piece of the cozy is worked sideways in double crochet and finished with a crocheted border. The squares are made separately, and the surface chain-stitching in bright contrasting colours adds extra detail.

Main piece

Using 4mm hook and purple, make 26ch.

Row 1: Miss 1ch (t-ch), work in dc to end (25 sts).

Row 2: 1ch (t-ch), dc to end.

Rep row 2 until work measures 1¾in (30cm). Do not break off yarn.

Border

Work 1 round of dc all round the four sides of the cover.

Fasten off.

Crochet squares

Using green, make 7ch.

Row 1: Miss 1ch (t-ch), dc to end. 6sts.

Row 2: 1ch (t-ch), dc to end.

Rep row 2 until work measures 1⅓in (3.5cm).

Make 12 identical squares.

Making up

Sew on the 12 green squares.

Work 4 vertical lines of chain stitch in red and 2 horizontal lines in yellow, then 3 vertical chain stitch lines in light blue followed by 6 small diamond shapes in mid-blue.

Attach the buttons, then make 3 chains of 8 sts each in 3 contrasting colours and sew on for button loops.

Sew the lining to the main cozy, allowing ¼in (1cm) all round for turning.

Note: see diagram (below) for placement of squares, embroidered lines, button loops and buttons.

Placement diagram

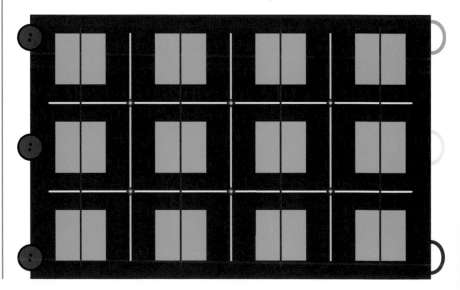

This design by Jane Greaves uses tapestry-style crochet in an innovative way to produce a tree design. Branches and coffee berries are embroidered on the fabric.

Straight from the tree

Materials

Rowan wool cotton DK (123yds/113m per 50g ball)
1 x 50g ball in 901 Citron (light green)
Debbie Bliss cashmerino DK (120yds/110m per 50g ball)
1 x 50g ball in 18011 Green (dark green)
Oddments of brown and red DK yarn
A 3mm (USC2-D/3:UK11) crochet hook

Tension

21 sts and 25 rows to 4cm (10cm) in dc using 3mm hook
Use larger or smaller hook to obtain correct tension

Special techniques

Tapestry crochet (see instructions)
French knots

Method

Work the cozy sideways in tapestry crochet, carrying the yarn not in use over the hook before working the next stitch. When changing colour, use the next colour to work the last loop of the stitch before, then pass the yarn used previously to the back of work.

Cozy

Using light green, make 36ch.
Turn the chain over and work 1dc into each stitch (36 sts).
Work 28 rows in dc.

Tree pattern

Work tree pattern as shown on chart over the next 34 rows, beginning at the left side and using dark green for leafy area and brown for trunk.
When chart is complete, work 6 rows more in light green (68 rows in total). Fasten off yarn.

Embroidery

Using brown, embroider branches in gaps in leafy area using back stitch. Using red, add french knots for the coffee berries.

Making up

Using light green, make 2 crochet chains each 50 sts long. Pass through the work near the top and bottom corners, tying in bows to secure around coffee pot.

Straight from the tree chart *36 sts x 34 rows*

Each square = 1 st and 1 row

Begin at the left side of chart

A 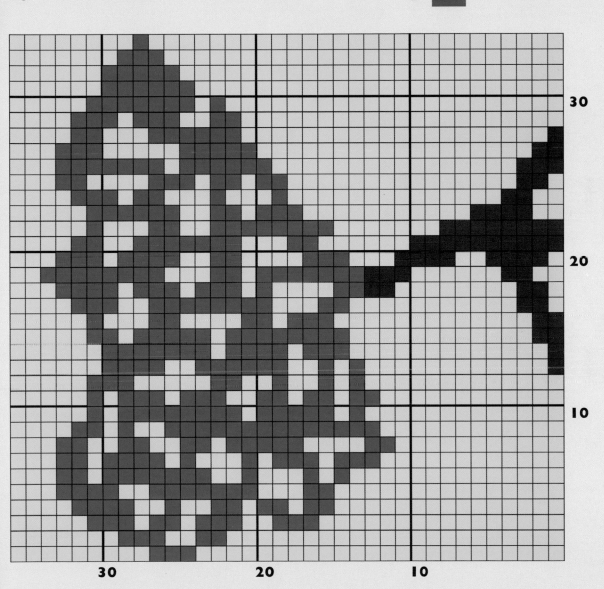 **C**

B

Strips of crochet are woven together for this highly-textured basket-weave design by Bernice Watkins. The bobble-style buttons are also made in crochet.

Woven strips

Materials

Any chunky yarn
1 x 50g ball maroon
A 5.5mm (USI/9:UK5) crochet hook
Darning needle

Tension

13 sts to 4in (10cm) over patt using 5.5mm hook
Each 3-row strip is approx 1¼in (3cm) high
Use larger or smaller hook to achieve correct tension

Method

This cozy is constructed by weaving together strips of crochet. The pieces are joined by working a single row of double crochet all round the outer edge, incorporating fastening loops.

Vertical strips (make 9)

Foundation chain: Make 21ch.
Row 1: Miss 1 ch (t-ch), 1 dc into each rem ch (20 sts).
Row 2: 2 ch (t-ch), 1 tr into each st to end.
Row 3: 1 ch (t-ch), 1 dc into each st to end.
Fasten off.

Horizontal strips (make 5)

Make 37 ch.
Row 1: Miss 1ch (t-ch), 1 dc into each rem ch st. 36 sts.
Row 2: 2ch (t-ch), 1 tr into each st to end.
Row 3: 1ch (t-ch), 1 dc into each st to end.
Fasten off.

Buttons (make 3)

4 ch, work 3 dtr into 1st chain, keeping last loop of each ch on the hook; pull yarn through all 4 loops to finish off the bobble.
Fasten off, leaving an end long enough to attach button.

Joining the strips

Weave strips together, over and under, remembering to work through both layers of fabric.
Beg at lower left corner, join strips by working 4dc across end of each strip. Turn the corner using 1ch, 4dc across first strip, 6ch for buttonhole loop, 4dc across next strip, 2dc to middle of next strip, 6ch for buttonhole loop, 2dc to end of strip, 4dc across next strip, 6ch for buttonhole loop, 4dc across last strip, 1ch to turn corner, 4dc across each strip, 1ch to turn corner, 4dc across each strip. Fasten off with a ss into first st.

Making up

Attach buttons ½in (1cm) from edge, level with buttonhole loops.

Fabulous yarn made from recycled sari silk in a mix of jewel colours inspired this design by Sarah Cox. Shiny sequins and gold medallions add to the air of over-the-top glamour.

Bollywood bling

Materials

Sari silk yarn (approx chunky weight)

1 × 100g ball

A pair of 5mm (US8:UK6) needles

Gold sequins

5 × gold metal coins

5 × small gold ring fasteners (optional)

3 × spherical metal bead drops (available from jewellery suppliers or haberdashery stores)

Sewing needle and toning thread

Short length of hook-and-loop fastener tape

Tension

14 sts and 17 rows to 4in (10cm) over st st using 5mm needles

Note: the yarn has very little stretch so it is important to check tension

Special techniques

Garter stitch (g-st)

Method

This cozy is knitted sideways in stocking stitch, with narrow borders at the top and lower edges. Tabs are knitted just before casting off, and fastened with hook-and-loop tape.

Cozy

Cast on 26 sts and work 3 rows in g-st.
Next row: Sl1, k to end.
Next row: Sl1, k1, p22, k2.
Rep last 2 rows until cozy measures 11¾in (30cm) or length to reach round coffee jug.

Tabs

Next row: K4, turn.
Work 4 rows g-st on these 4 sts, then cast them off.
Rejoin yarn to rem sts.
Cast off 7 sts, k4.
Work 4 rows g-st on these 5 sts, then cast them off.
Rejoin yarn to rem sts.
Cast off 7 sts, k4.
Work 4 rows g-sts on these 4 sts, then cast them off.

Tip

If you cannot find metal coins, substitute a few larger sequins. Buttons may be used instead of metal bead drops if preferred.

Making up

Sew in ends of yarn. Using sewing thread, attach sequins randomly to cozy. Attach gold coins using small pliers and the ring fasteners or sew in place. Cut 3 small pieces of hook-and-loop fastener tape and attach to back of tabs and cover, lining up carefully. Attach bead drops to front of tabs.

Alternate panels of stocking stitch and textured rice stitch lend interest to this design by Anita Ursula Nycs, which is embellished with buttons and chain stitch embroidery.

Buttoned up

Materials

Any Aran weight yarn

1 x 100g ball in cream

Oddment of brown yarn for embroidery

A pair of 5mm (US8:UK6) needles

4.5mm (US7:UK7) crochet hook

9 buttons (3 for fastening and 6 for decoration)

A piece of purple fabric 7in x 12in (18cm x 31cm)

Darning needle

Sewing needle and coordinating thread

Tension

18 sts and 24 rows to 4in (10cm) over st st using 5mm needles

Use larger or smaller needles to obtain correct tension

Special techniques

Stocking stitch

Rice stitch pattern: see instructions

Method

This cozy is worked in alternating panels of stocking stitch and textured rice stitch with added embroidery.

Cozy

Using 5mm needles and cream yarn, cast on 32 sts.

* Work in rice st for 2⅓in (6cm).

Rice stitch pattern

Row 1 (RS): (p1, k1) to end.

Row 2: Knit.

Rep these 2 rows for patt.

Work in st st for 2⅓in (6cm).

Rep from * once, then work in rice st for a further 2⅓in (6cm).

Cast off.

Making up

Attach 3 buttons to each st st panel, then embroider a chain stitch square around each button.

Attach the remaining buttons, evenly spaced, to one of the short edges. Using the 4.5mm hook and cream, make crochet chain fastenings and attach to the opposite edge, to correspond with the buttons.

Border

Using the 4.5mm hook and cream yarn, work a row of dc along each of the longer sides of the knitted piece. Sew in any loose ends.

Lining

Sew the fabric to the back of the knitted piece, allowing ¼in (6mm) for turning.

This saucy red-and-black design by Charmaine Fletcher evokes the sophistication of the bright young things who frequented fashionable coffee houses from the beginning of the last century. Oh là là!

Café society

Materials
Hayfield Bonus DK (306yds/280m per 100g ball)
1 x 100g ball in 977 Signal red
1 x 100g ball in 965 Black
3 x ½in (1cm) black buttons (Coats 1030A)
A pair of 4mm (US6:UK8:) needles
A 2.5mm (USC/2:UK12:) crochet hook
A piece of red felt 6¾in x 11¾in (17 x 30cm)
Darning needle
Sewing needle and coordinating thread
Dressmaker's pins

Tension
21 sts and 30 rows to 4in (10cm) over stocking stitch using 4mm needles
Use larger or smaller needles to obtain correct tension.

Special techniques
Thumb method cast-on
Moss stitch (m-st)

Method

This cozy is knitted in one piece from top to bottom with moss stitch edges to give a firm border. Ruffles are made separately and added, and corset-style lacing is used to fasten the buttons.

Cozy

Using 4mm needles and black yarn, cast on 62 sts using the thumb method.

Row 1: Purl.

Row 2: Change to red and k one row.

Row 3: M-st 4, (k4, p1) to last 4 sts, m-st 4.

Row 4: M-st 4, k to last 4 sts, m-st 4.

Rep rows 3–4 for patt with m-st border.

Cont as set until piece measures 6¼in (16cm), finishing with a RS row.

Next row: Change to black and p to end.

Next row: Cast off k-wise.

Ruffles (make 2)

Using 4mm needles and red, cast on 120 sts.

Row 1: (K2tog) to end (60 sts).

Row 2: (P2tog) to end (30 sts).

Row 3: Change to black and k to end.

Row 4: Cast off using black, leaving a long tail for sewing.

Making up

Sew in loose ends. Pin the ruffles into place (see photograph for reference) and attach to cozy.

Buttons

Cut a 12in (30cm) length of red wool and separate the strands. Take one strand, double over and make a loop knot to start. Spacing evenly, attach the top, middle and lower buttons, creating a shank to fit through the lacing.

Corset-style lacing loops (make 3)

Using the 2.5mm hook and black, make 16ch, ss into 7th ch, make 5ch, ss into 1st ch to form a 'figure-of-eight'. Fasten off, leaving a long tail. Attach the lacing loops to the opposite edge, to correspond with the buttons.

Lining

Pin the felt to the back of the knitted piece and sew into place.

Tip
Instead of using felt for lining, knit a second piece using black and following the instructions for the main cozy.

Scrummy buns and yummy pastels are a mouthwatering combination in this design by Frankie Brown that looks almost good enough to eat. Pretty pastel buttons add extra interest.

Coffee and cake

Materials
Rowan Cashsoft DK (142yds/130m per 50g ball)
1 x 50g ball in 520 Bloom (M)
Small amounts of DK yarn in cream, yellow, blue, green, lilac and brown
A pair of 3.25mm (US3:UK10) needles
4 x ½in (1.5cm) buttons
24 assorted buttons for decoration

Tension
25 sts and 35 rows to 4in (10cm) over st st using 3.25mm needles
Use larger or smaller needles to achieve correct tension

Special techniques
Reverse stocking stitch (rev st-st): use the reverse side of stocking stitch as the right side

Method

The main piece is knitted first, beginning and ending with rev st st with the main panel in st st. Stitches are picked up and worked in g-st for the button and buttonhole bands. The cake pieces are made, assembled and sewn on and buttons are added for extra decoration.

Main piece

Using M, cast on 70 sts.

Beg with a purl row, work 4 rows in reverse stocking stitch for top edge.

Next row: Beg with a k row, work 55 rows in stocking stitch.

Now work 4 rows in rev st st for top edge, beg with a knit row.

Cast off k-wise.

Note: the top and bottom of the sides should be allowed to curl naturally and worked as one layer.

Button bands

With RS facing pick up and k 40 sts along one side.

Working on the first 6 sts only, work 6 rows g-st and cast off.

Rejoin yarn and cast off the next 6 sts.

Working on the next 16 sts, work 6 rows g-st and cast off.

Rejoin yarn and cast off the next 6 sts.

Working on the last 6 sts, work 6 rows g-st and cast off.

Buttonhole bands

With RS facing pick up and k 40 sts along the other side, allowing the top and bottom to curl as before. Work 2 rows in g-st on the first 6 sts only.

Next row: K2, cast off 2 sts, k2.

Next row: K2, cast on 2 sts, k2.

Work 2 more rows in g-st and cast off.

Rejoin yarn and cast off the next 6 sts.

Working on the next 16 sts, work 2 rows g-st.

Next row: K3, cast off 2 sts, k6, cast off 2 sts, k3.

Next row: K3, cast on 2 sts, k6, cast on 2 sts, k3.

Work 2 more rows in g-st and cast off.

Rejoin yarn and cast off the next 6 sts.

Working on the last 6 sts, work 2 rows g-st.

Next row: K2, cast off 2 sts, k2.

Next row: K2, cast on 2 sts, k2.

Work 2 more rows in g-st.

Cast off.

Cakes (make 4)

Using chosen colour, cast on 9 sts.

Row 1: (P1, k1) to end.

Row 2: (K1, p1) to end.

Row 3: P1, k1, (p1, m1, k1) twice, p1, k1, p1.

Row 4: K1, p1, (k1, p2) twice, k1, p1, k1.

Row 5: P1, m1, k1, (p1, k2) twice, p1, m1, k1, p1.

Row 6: (K1, p2) 4 times, k1.

Row 7: P1, k2, (p1, m1, k2) twice, p1, k2, p1.

Row 8: K1, p2, (k1, p3) twice, k1, p2, k1.

Row 9: P1, m1, k2, (p1, k3) twice, p1, m1, k2, p1 (17 sts).

Cake

Change to brown.

Row 1: Knit.

Row 2 (and every even row): Purl.

Row 3: Ssk, k to last 2 sts, k2tog.

Row 5: Ssk, k to last 2 sts, k2tog.

Row 7: Ssk, k2, ssk, k1, k2tog, k2, k2tog (9 sts).

Cast off p-wise.

Icing

Using cream yarn cast on 16 sts.

Row 1 (and every odd row): Purl.

Row 2: K2, (m1, k1) twice, (k2tog) 4 times, (m1, k1) twice, k2.

Row 4: Ssk, k3, ssk, k2, k2tog, k3, k2tog (12 sts).

Row 6: Ssk, k1, ssk, k2, k2tog, k1, k2tog (8 sts).
Row 8: (ssk) twice, (k2tog) twice. Thread yarn through rem 4 sts and fasten off.

Sweets

Using 'sweet' colour cast on 2 sts.
Row 1 and every odd row: Purl.
Row 2: K1, m1, k1.
Row 4: K1, m1, k1, m1, k1.
Row 6: Knit.
Row 8: Ssk, k1, k2tog.
Row 10: Sl1, k2tog, psso and fasten off.
Work running stitches round the edge of the knitted piece and gather, then knot the cast on and cast off ends together.

Making up

Arrange the cakes on the cozy and sew in place. Attach the icing and the sweets, and use the assorted buttons to fill the spaces between the cakes. Attach the buttons to the button bands to correspond with buttonholes.

A naked coffee pot!

Techniques

How to make your prized pot decent

Measurements

The instructions given are for a standard six-cup coffee jug as shown. Each cozy measures approximately 6¾ x 11¾in (17 x 30cm). If your jug is a little larger than this, try changing the needles for a bigger size and working a few more rows to make the sides longer. If it is smaller, a change to smaller needles may bring down the dimensions sufficiently.

Tension

Tension is important as just a slight difference can have a noticeable effect on the size of the finished cozy. If you are a new knitter, it is a good idea to start a habit that will save a lot of time in the end: work a swatch using the chosen yarn and needles. These can be labelled and filed for future reference. The tension required is given at the beginning of each pattern.

Materials and equipment

Needles and hooks

Most of the designs in this book are worked back and forth on standard knitting needles. Bamboo needles are useful if you are using a rough-textured yarn as they are very smooth and will help to prevent snags. You may also need double-pointed needles.

Where crochet hooks are used, these are standard metal hooks that are widely available.

Yarn

Cozies may be made in a huge variety of yarns. Wool or wool-mix yarns have the best insulating properties, but cotton or silk are also good. If you are using acrylic yarn, you may prefer to choose one of the thicker designs, or one that has a lining. Cozies are also an ideal way to use up oddments of yarn.

Substituting yarn

It is relatively simple to substitute different yarns for any of the projects in this book. One way to do this is to work out how many wraps per inch (wpi) the yarn produces (see table left). It is important to check tension, so begin by working a tension swatch. Then wind the yarn closely, in a single layer, round a rule or similar object, and count how many 'wraps' it produces to an inch (2.5cm). For a successful result, choose a yarn that produces twice, or slightly more than twice, the number of wraps per inch as there are stitches per inch in the tension swatch.

Tension required	Number of wraps per inch produced by yarn
8 sts per in (4-ply/fingering)	16–18 wraps per inch
6.5 sts per in (DK/sport)	13–14 wraps per inch
5.5 sts per in (Chunky/worsted)	11–12 wraps per inch

Knitting techniques

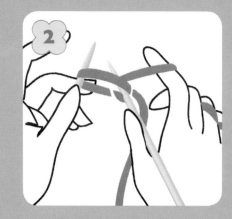

Simple cast-on

1 Form a slip knot on the left needle. Insert the right needle into the loop and wrap yarn round it as shown.

2 Pull the yarn through the first loop to create a new one.

3 Slide it on to the left-hand needle.

There are now 2 sts on the left needle. Continue in this way until you have the required number of sts.

Cable cast-on

For a firmer edge, cast on the first 2 sts as shown above. When casting on the third and subsequent sts, insert the needle *between* the cast-on sts on the left needle, wrap the yarn round and pull through to create a loop. Slide the loop on to the left needle. Repeat to end.

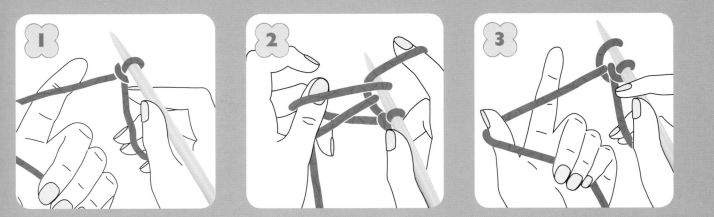

Thumb method cast-on

1 Make a slip knot some way from the end of the yarn and place on the needle. Pull the knot tight.

2 Hold needle in right hand and wrap the loose tail end round the left thumb, from front to back. Push the needle point through the thumb loop from front to back. Wind ball end of yarn round needle from left to right.

3 Pull the loop through thumb loop, then remove thumb. Gently pull the new loop tight using the tail yarn. Rep until the desired number of sts are on the needle.

Knit stitch

1 Hold the needle with the cast-on sts in your left hand. Place the tip of the empty right needle into the first st and wrap the yarn round as for casting on.

2 Pull the yarn through to create a new loop.

3 Slip the newly-made st on to the right needle.

Continue in the same way for each st on the left-hand needle.

To start a new row, turn the work to swap the needles and repeat steps.

Purl stitch

1 Hold the yarn at the front of the work as shown.

2 Place the right needle into the first st from front to back. Wrap the yarn round the needle in an anti-clockwise direction as shown.

3 Bring the needle back through the st and pull through.

Ⓐ Garter stitch (g-st)

Knit every row.

Ⓑ Stocking stitch (st st)

Knit on RS rows and purl on WS rows.

Ⓒ Moss stitch (m-st)

With an even number of sts:
Row 1: (k1, p1) to end.
Row 2: (p1, k1) to end.
Rep rows 1 and 2 for pattern.

With an odd number of sts:
Row 1: *k1, p1, rep from * to
last st, k1.
Rep to form pattern.

Ⓓ Single (1 x 1) rib

With an even number of sts:
Row 1: *K1, p1* rep to end.
Rep for each row.

With an odd number of sts:
Row 1: *K1, p1, rep from * to
last st, k1.
Row 2: *P1, k1, rep from * to
last st, p1.

Ⓔ Double (2 x 2) rib

Row 1: *K2, p2, rep from * to end.
Rep for each row.

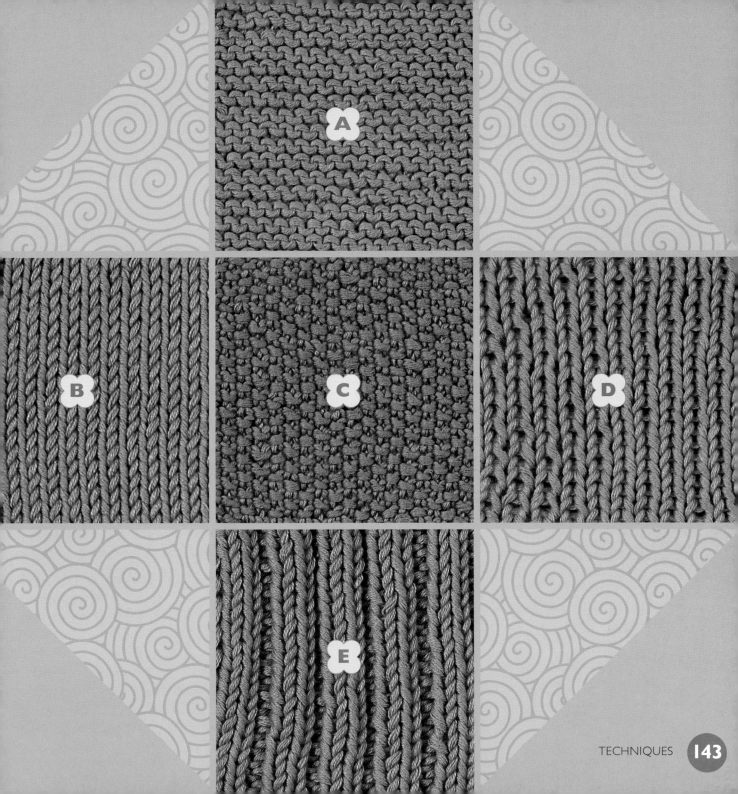

Colour knitting

Intarsia

Blocks of colour are created by using the intarsia technique of twisting the yarns together at the back of the work with each colour change (see diagram below). It is better to use bobbins than whole balls to prevent tangling. They are smaller and can hang at the back of the work out of the way. Once they are finished, the ends are woven in at the back. Pressing under a damp cloth will help neaten any distorted stitches.

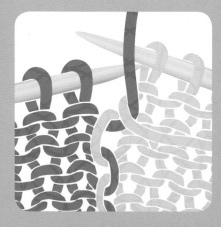

Fairisle

Fairisle knitting uses the stranding technique, which involves picking up and dropping yarns as they are needed. Unlike intarsia, they are then carried across the row. Loops are formed along the back of the work, but these should not exceed about 5 sts in length. Make sure the loops are of even tension or the fabric may pucker.

1 Begin knitting with the first colour (A) which is dropped when you need to incorporate the second (B). To pick up A again bring it under B and knit again.

2 To pick up B again, drop A and bring B over A, then knit again.

Reading charts

Most charts are shown in squares, with each square representing one stitch. Charts are usually marked in sections of ten stitches, which makes counting easier.

When working in stocking stitch on straight needles, read the chart from right to left on knit (RS) rows and from left to right on purl (WS) rows. Check carefully after every purl row to make sure that the pattern stitches are in the correct position.

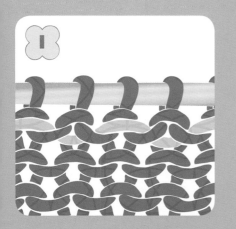

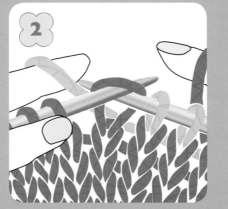

Cable stitch

With the help of a cable needle, these decorative stitches are quite straightforward. Stitches are slipped on to the needle and then knitted later to create the twists.

Front cable worked over 4 sts (cab4f)

1 Slip the next 2 sts on to a cable needle and hold in front of work.

2 Knit the next 2 stitches from the left needle as normal, then knit the 2 sts from the cable needle.

Back cable worked over 4sts (cab4b)

Slip the next 2 sts on to a cable needle and hold at back of work.

Knit the next 2 sts from the left needle as normal, then knit the 2 sts from the cable needle.

Casting off

1 Knit 2 sts on to the right needle, then slip the first st over the second st and let it drop off the needle (1 st remains).

2 Knit another st so you have 2 sts on the right needle again.

Rep process until there is only 1 st on the left needle. Break yarn and thread through rem st to fasten off.

Sewing up

Place the pieces to be joined on a flat surface laid together side-by-side with right sides towards you. Using matching yarn, thread a needle back and forth with small, straight stitches. The stitches form a ladder between the two pieces of fabric, creating a flat, secure seam. This technique is usually known as mattress stitch.

Stocking stitch joins

The edges of stocking stitch tend to curl, so it may be tricky to join. The best way to join it is to use mattress stitch to pick up the bars between the columns of stitches.

Working upwards or downwards according to preference, secure the yarn to one of the pieces you want to join. Place the edges of the work together and pick up a bar from one side, then pick up the corresponding bar from the opposite side. Repeat. After a few stitches, pull gently on the yarn and the two sides will come together in a seam that is almost invisible. Take care to stay in the same column all the way. Do not pull the stitches tight at first as you will not be able to see what you are doing.

Garter stitch joins

It is easier to join garter stitch as it has a firm edge and lies flat. Place the edges of the work together, right side up, and see where the stitches line up. Pick up the bottom loops of the stitches on one side of the work and the top loops of the stitches on the other side. After a few stitches, pull gently on the yarn. The stitches should lock together and lie completely flat. The inside of the join should look the same as the outside.

Crochet techniques

Chain stitch (ch)

1 With hook in right hand and yarn resting over middle finger of left hand, pull yarn taut. Take hook under, then over yarn.

2 Pull the hook and yarn through the loop while holding slip knot steady. Rep to form a foundation row of chain stitch (ch).

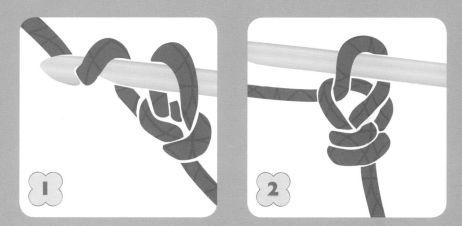

Double crochet (dc)

1 Place hook into a st. Wrap yarn round hook and draw the loop back through the work towards you.

2 There should now be two loops on the hook. Wrap yarn round hook again, then draw through both loops, leaving one loop on the hook (one double crochet (dc) now complete. Rep to continue row.

Stitch tips

Chain stitch (**A**) is the usual base
for other crochet stitches and is also useful
for making simple ties. Double crochet (**B**)
produces a dense fabric that is ideal for
lining, and single rows are ideal for edging.
Crochet worked in half-treble (**C**) and
treble (**D**) stitch has a more open weave.

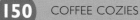

Half-treble (h-tr)

Wrap yarn round hook, then place into a stitch. Wrap yarn round hook, then draw the loop through (3 loops now on hook). Wrap yarn round hook again and draw through the 3 loops (one loop remains on hook).

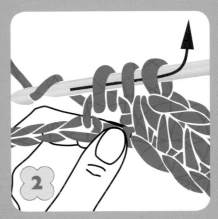

Treble (tr)

Follow instructions for half treble until there are 3 loops on the hook. Catch yarn with hook and draw through 2 of the loops, then catch yarn again and draw through rem 2 loops.

Finishing touches

Blanket stitch

This is an ideal way of finishing felted edges to stop them from fraying, and can also be used when adding appliqué designs to your work.

Work from left to right. The twisted edge should lie on the outer edge of the fabric to form a raised line. Bring needle up at point **A**, down at **B** and up at **C** with thread looped under the needle. Pull through. Take care to tighten the stitches equally. Repeat to the right. Fasten the last loop by taking a small stitch along the lower line.

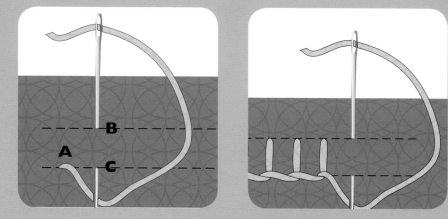

Making an I-cord

Using double-pointed needles, cast on the required number of stitches. Do not turn; slide stiches to the opposite end of the needle, then take the yarn firmly across the back of work. Knit stitches again. Repeat to desired length. Cast off.

Abbreviations

approx	approximately	**LH**	left-hand side	**sl**	slip		
ch	chain stitch	**M**	metre OR Main (colour)	**ssk**	slip 1 st k-wise, slip 1 st p-wise; knit these 2 sts together through the back of the loops		
cont	continue	**M1**	make 1 stitch				
cm(s)	centimetre(s)	**M1L**	make 1 stitch slanting left (left increase)	**ssp**	slip 1 st knitwise, slip 1 stitch purlwise, then purl both stitches together		
dc	double crochet	**M1R**	make 1 stitch slanting right (right increase)				
d-g st	double garter stitch (2 rounds p, 2 rounds k)	**mm**	millimetres	**st(s)**	stitch(es)		
dtr	double treble	**m-st**	moss stitch	**st st**	stocking stitch		
DK	double knitting	**p**	purl	**T3L**	twist 3 sts left		
foll	following	**patt**	pattern	**t-ch**	turning chain		
g	gramme(s)	**p2tog**	purl two stitches together	**tog**	together		
g-st	garter stitch			**tr**	treble		
htr	half treble	**psso**	pass slipped stitch over	*****	work instructions following *, then repeat as directed		
inc	increase by working twice into the stitch	**p-wise**	with needles positioned as if to purl				
in(s)	inch(es)	**rem**	remaining	**( )**	repeat instructions inside brackets as directed		
k	knit	**rev st st**	reverse stocking stitch				
k-wise	with needles positioned as if to knit	**R**	right	**WS**	wrong side of work		
		RS	right side of work	**yb**	yarn back		
k2tog	knit two sts together	**sk**	skip	**yd(s)**	yard (s)		
L	left	**ss**	slip stitch	**yf**	yarn forward		

Conversions

Needle sizes

UK	Metric	US
14	2mm	0
13	2.5mm	1
12	2.75mm	2
11	3mm	–
10	3.25mm	3
–	3.5mm	4
9	3.75mm	5
8	4mm	6
7	4.5mm	7
6	5mm	8
5	5.5mm	9
4	6mm	10
3	6.5mm	10.5
2	7mm	10.5
1	7.5mm	11
0	8mm	11
00	9mm	13
000	10mm	15

UK/US yarn weights

UK	US
2–ply	Lace
3–ply	Fingering
4–ply	Sport
Double knitting	Light worsted
Aran	Fisherman/worsted
Chunky	Bulky
Super chunky	Extra bulky

Index

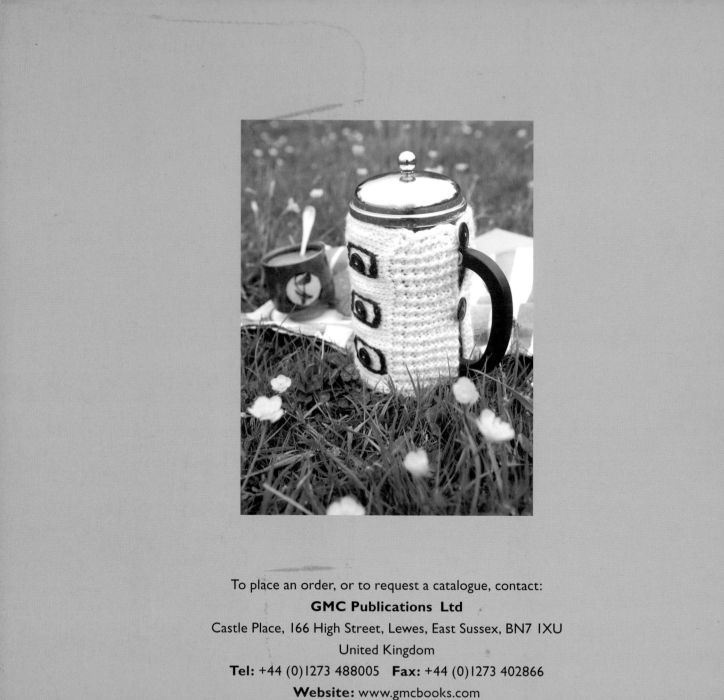

To place an order, or to request a catalogue, contact:

GMC Publications Ltd

Castle Place, 166 High Street, Lewes, East Sussex, BN7 IXU

United Kingdom

Tel: +44 (0)1273 488005   **Fax:** +44 (0)1273 402866

Website: www.gmcbooks.com

Orders by credit card are accepted